How the Angels
Got Their Wings

Anthony DeStefano

Illustrated by

ANTONIO JAVIER CAPARO

SOPHIA
INSTITUTE PRESS

Printed in the United States of America.

Sophia Institute Press®
Box 5284, Manchester, NH 03108
1-800-888-9344

www.SophiaInstitute.com

ISBN: 978-1-64413-517-4

Library of Congress Control Number: 2022932593

This book is dedicated with gratitude
and affection to my guardian angel.

—Anthony DeStefano

Who IS that angel that we see perched atop the Christmas tree?

And how can angels fly so high,
soaring through the snowy sky?

And why do angels dress in white?
And do the angels ever fight?

Who made the angels? Any clue?
He who made them made YOU too!

So listen, children, gather near.
Listen now, and you will hear
an ancient tale that's true and thrilling,
sacred, stirring, sometimes chilling.

There isn't any other story
filled with so much grace and glory
as the song sweet Heaven sings
of how the angels got their wings.

Our God is King; He reigns above—
the source of life, of joy, of love.
He made the moon, the stars, the sun
and rested when His work was done.

But when He made this grand creation,
before He laid the earth's foundation,
He made great spirits full of might,
invisible yet formed of light.

Some stayed good, and some turned bad;
one of them was proud and mad—
mad that HE was not the king,
mad at God for everything.

The devil, Satan—that's his name
(either one means just the same)—
led some angels to rebel.
God cast those demons down to Hell.

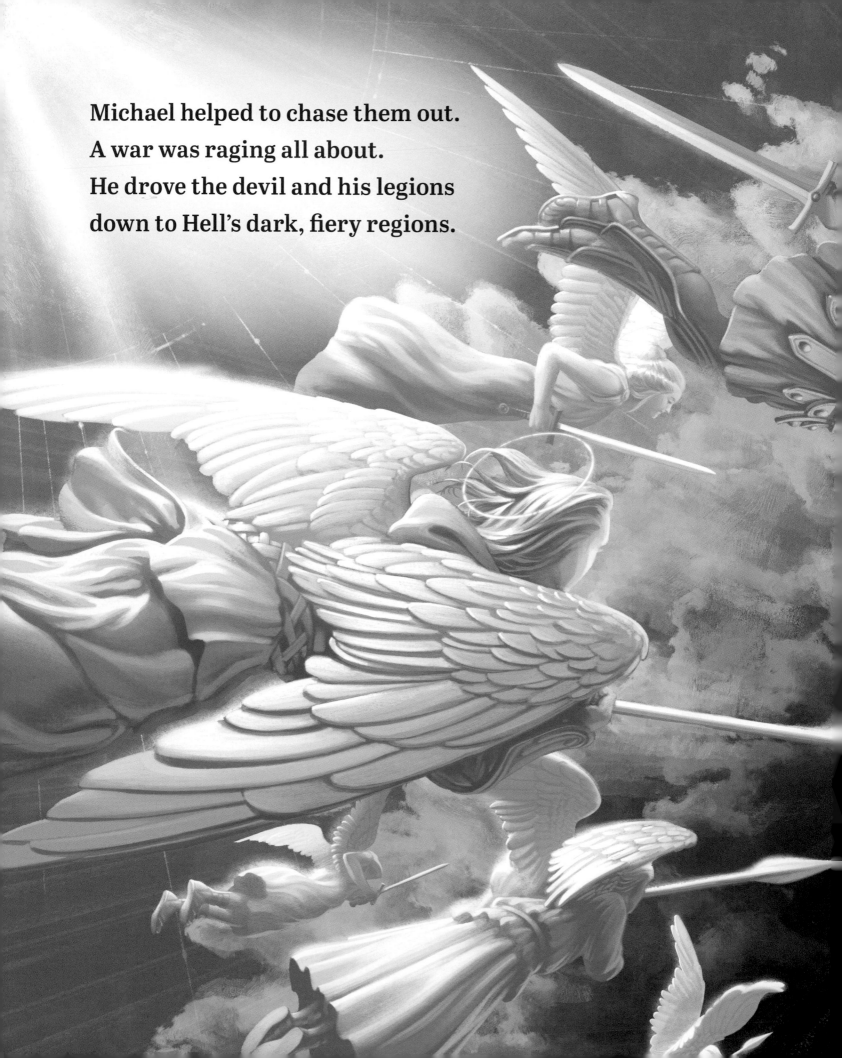

Michael helped to chase them out.
A war was raging all about.
He drove the devil and his legions
down to Hell's dark, fiery regions.

St. Michael can protect us too
from all the sinful things we do,
helping us to fight temptation,
battling for our souls' salvation.

"Archangel" is St. Michael's title.
Three of them are in the Bible;
three who carry out God's plan;
three who serve both God and Man.

St. Raphael cured Tobit's blindness,
healing him with God's great kindness.
He put some oil on Tobit's eyes,
and Tobit saw the bright sun rise.

St. Raphael can help us heal,
No matter how unwell we feel.
He lifts our spirits when we're low
and helps our faith in God to grow.

St. Gabriel was sent to Earth
to herald Our Lord Jesus' birth.
He looked at Mary's shining face
and told her she was full of grace.

St. Gabriel can help us speak,
even if we're shy or meek,
and spread the news to everyone
about the Lord, God's only Son.

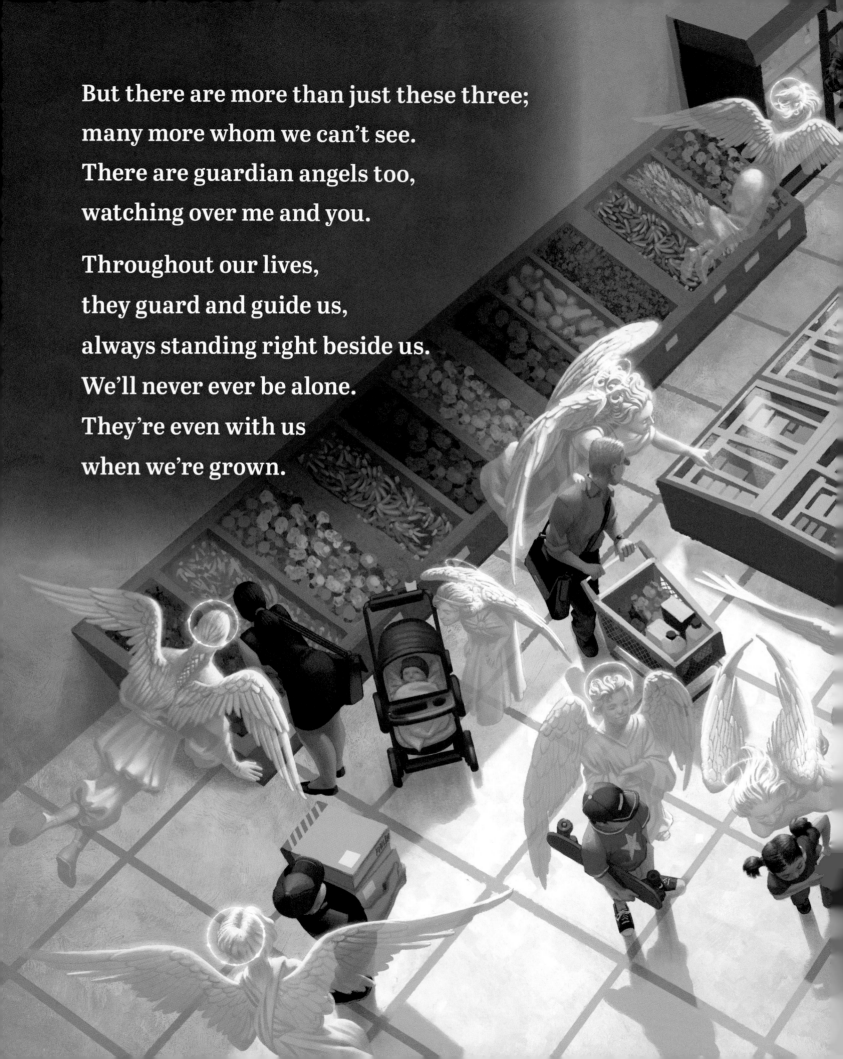

But there are more than just these three;
many more whom we can't see.
There are guardian angels too,
watching over me and you.

Throughout our lives,
they guard and guide us,
always standing right beside us.
We'll never ever be alone.
They're even with us
when we're grown.

There are angels EVERYWHERE!
We can't see them, but they're there!

Angels by the Christmas manger;
angels saving those in danger;

angels dressed up in disguise;

angels there when someone dies;

Millions up in Heaven bringing
blessings down to all the living;
bringing hope and consolation
where there's death and desolation.

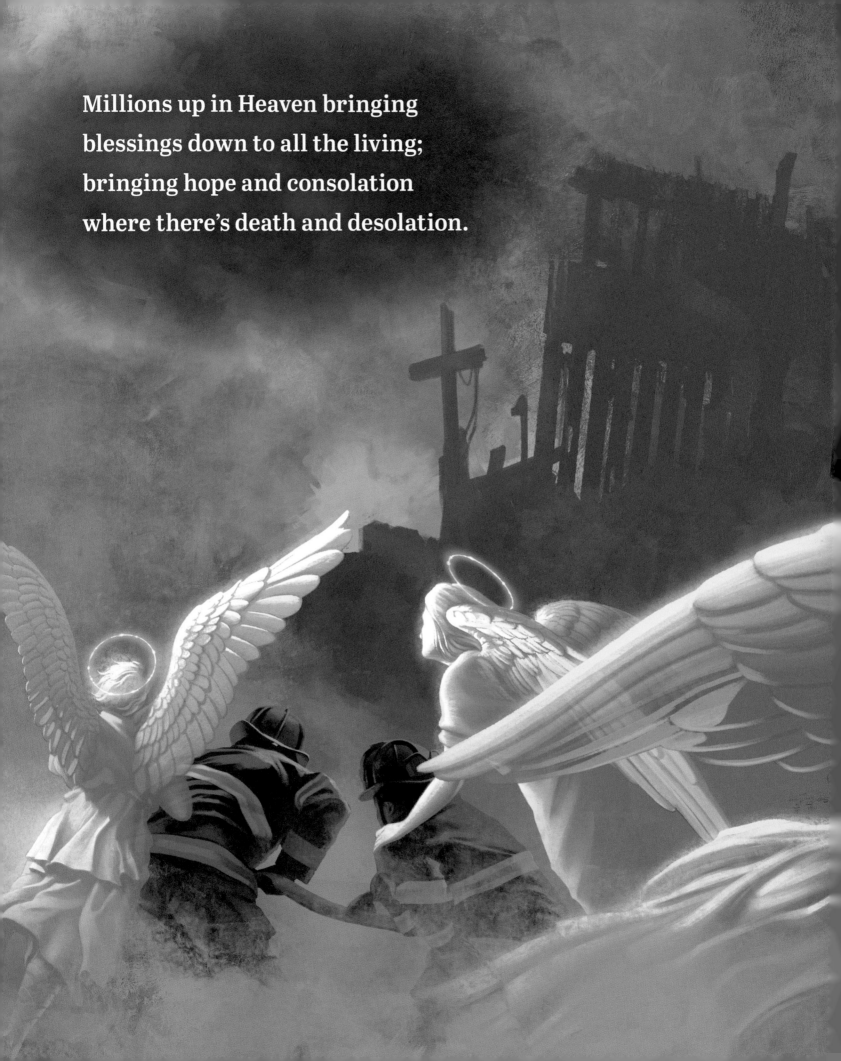

But if you really want to search,
look for angels in your church.

That's where angels gather most—
before the consecrated Host.

God made angels long ago.
They serve in Heaven, and below.
He gave them wings so they could fly
across the vast and sun-filled sky.

Sweet messengers from paradise,
they teach us love and sacrifice.
They fly from Heaven to the ground,
invisible, without a sound.

But you can sense them in the air—
especially alone at prayer.
They're present in so many things;
in summers, winters, falls, and springs;

like when a children's choir sings,
or when a morning church bell rings,
or in a mother's love that clings,

or in the joy a story brings ...
of how the angels got their wings.

A PRAYER
TO ALL ANGELS

All of you angels of God everywhere,
won't you please listen to my little prayer?

St. Michael, protect me from evil today.
Chase Satan and all of his demons away.

St. Raphael, cure me from illness and stress.
Grant me God's healing and true faithfulness.

St. Gabriel, make all my speaking devout.
Then give me the courage and strength to speak out.

Guardian angel, free me from fear.
Protect me from danger whenever it's near.

Immaculate Mary, the angels' great queen,
command all these powerful spirits unseen
to help me in this life, and then when I'm done,
to lead me to Heaven to be with your Son.

Oh, thank you, dear angels, for all that you do.
Please know I'm so grateful
and that I LOVE YOU!